Finding Grace

a Parable

By David L. Erickson

GOLD 'N' HONEY BOOKS   SISTERS, OREGON

FINDING GRACE

published by GOLD 'N' HONEY BOOKS

a division of Multnomah Publishers, Inc.

© 1998 by David L. Erickson

Illustrations © 1998 by David L. Erickson

Design by Open Door Design

International Standard Book Number: 1-57673-245-2

Scripture quotations are from: *The Holy Bible*, New International Version

© 1973, 1984 by International Bible Society,

used by permission of Zondervan Publishing House

Printed in Hong Kong

For information:

MULTNOMAH PUBLISHERS, INC.

POST OFFICE BOX 1720

SISTERS, OREGON 97759

Library of Congress Cataloging-in-Publication Data:
Erickson, David (David L.)
Finding Grace / by David Erickson; illustrated by David Erickson.
　　　　　p.　　cm.
　　　Summary: Love keeps Charlie looking for the lost butterfly Grace, although
he faces blinding winds, an endless cornfield, an angry bull, and a dark forest.
　　　ISBN 1-57673-245-2 (alk. paper)
　　　[1. Butterflies—Fiction. 2. Lost and found possessions—
Fiction.] I.Title.
PZ7.E725545Fi 1998
[E]—dc21
　　　　　　　　　　　　　　　　　　　　　　　　　　97-45002
　　　　　　　　　　　　　　　　　　　　　　　　　　　CIP
　　　　　　　　　　　　　　　　　　　　　　　　　　　AC

98 99 00 01 02 03 — 10 9 8 7 6 5 4 3 2 1

To my parents

Proverbs 17:6

"Suppose one of you
has a hundred sheep and
loses one of them..."

LUKE 15:4

Ninety-eight...ninety-nine...
one hundred butterflies." Charlie grinned. "Yep, I got 'em all!"
It wasn't easy to count all the colorful butterflies that flitted around
his father's wildflower garden. But that's what
made it fun. Not only did Charlie count them every day,
he knew them each by name. There was a Spike
and a Rebecca, and even a Mumfreys and a Crabapple,
and lots of other names too.

And there was Grace.

Early every morning, before chores, Charlie dashed outside
to the butterfly garden to count his butterflies. He loved these
butterflies. They were of all sorts of shapes
and colors.

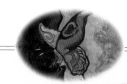

Late one morning, while all the butterflies were playing a big game of tag, Charlie and his father both stood atop a high hill. The father placed his big hand on Charlie's shoulder and pointed to the far-off horizon. Charlie frowned. Something out there was very wrong.

His father gently squeezed Charlie's shoulder, and with concern in his voice he said, "You ought to get your butterflies inside the house then, Charlie, and hurry, son, that windstorm is a big-un!"

Charlie could see that it was a mighty windstorm, shaking to bits everything that lay in its path, and it was headed right for their farm.

Wasting no time, Charlie called his butterflies together and began to
lead a long, colorful line of fluttering wings up his front walk
and straight into his house.

"What's going on?" they asked each other with excitement.
"What's happening?" Not a single butterfly knew for sure,
but just the same, they kept their eyes on Charlie.

"Hurry up now! Hurry up now!" Charlie shouted. He knew he
sounded cross, but the wind was growing, and the trees were swaying.
And Charlie was very upset. He loved each and every butterfly, from
the little tiny elfins to the huge swallowtails. He wasn't willing to let
anything happen to a single one of them!

Once inside, all the butterflies lined themselves up along
the edges of the windows.
They watched the farmyard outside, and waited.

In the next instant, it looked as if every fan ever made had been turned on high. The awesome, terrible wind washed over the farmyard like a tidal wave of air. It bent trees as if they were rubber and pushed on the house until it groaned and creaked.

Inside, no one said a word. They just watched with wide-eyed wonder. Then suddenly the butterflies at the kitchen window began to shriek with fear. There, being swept away by a mighty gust, was their friend Grace! She was outside in this horrible storm!

Charlie shot out the door. "Oh, no! Oh, no!"

The wind had already grabbed Grace and thrown her high above the farm~higher than she'd ever been before. But not for long. Whooooshh! She was thrown back down to earth. She continued to fly bravely, racing just inches above the grass, searching for a place to hide. But she was no match for the strength of the wind. She was dragged into and out of prickly bushes. She was thrown against the brick chimney and even smacked into the living-room window. Whap!
The butterflies in the living room watched in horror.

"There she is," they all shouted. "There she goes.
Oh, watch out for that bush, Grace!"

"Where are you, Grace?" shouted Charlie in a dizzy panic. "Where are you?" He searched the garden, along the fence, and around the house. He searched the barn and the silo. He looked in the trees and in the bushes~and the whole while, the roaring windstorm threw dust and dirt into his eyes and up his nose.

Inside the house, the butterflies were in a frenzy! They flew wildly about, colliding into each other again and again. They zipped from window to window, hoping to catch a glimpse of their lost friend.

"Excuse me," said Rebecca.

"Watch it!" cried Spike.

"Look out!" snapped Crabapple. "I was going there!"

Outside, Charlie wiped the dirt from his eyes and began to cry.

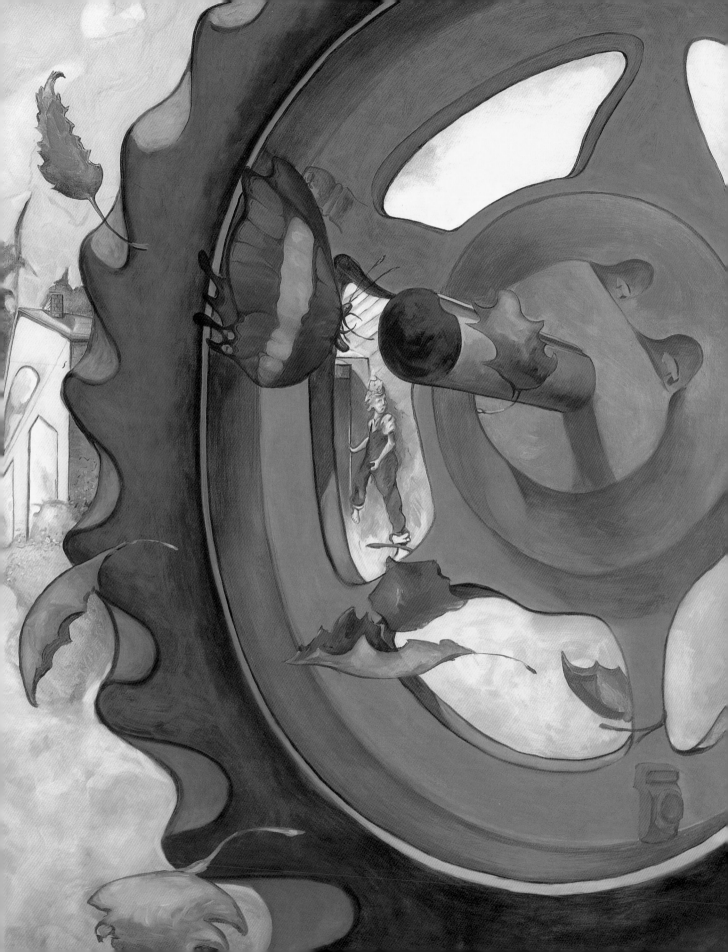

SWOOOOSHH! The howling wind swooped up Grace and whipped her into the pig shed. An old sow was hunkered down to escape the howling storm. But when she saw Grace spinning wildly above her, she was so alarmed that she leaped to her feet with a squeal that disturbed every pig in the shed!

Panicked pigs jumped to their feet oinking and snorting and squealing and plowing into each other. Poor Grace. All she could do was grab the snout of a bucking boar and ride him like a rodeo cowboy.

But the bucking boar burst past the frantic pigs and through the open sty and back outside. Back into the wind and...swoosh! Grace was back in the air!

But this time Charlie saw her. "I see you, Grace!" he cried. "I see you!" No sooner were the words out of his mouth than a big gust of wind blew a fistful of dirt smack into Charlie's face. He fell to his knees, rubbing his eyes. Meanwhile, Grace was swept far away by the wind, even beyond the cornfield.

Charlie bolted back into the house and looked to his father.
"Yes," said his father, "go and get her, Charlie!"

So Charlie bolted back out the door and headed in the direction
that the wind had last taken her. He didn't even slow down when he
met up with a creek. In he went, up to his belly button, and oooh,
was it chilly! It took his breath away, but he kept going.
The wind whipped up stinging sprays of water, smacking them right
into his face. Then splaaashh! The bottom of the creek
dropped away and Charlie went completely under. He took
a big breath and swam for the other side.

He climbed out on the other bank and paused. He shook enough
of the creek from his overalls to water half the cornfield that
lay before him. He stared at the rows and rows of corn.
The field seemed to stretch on forever~
both to his left and to his right.

Charlie plunged into the first row and ran a few feet, then stopped
and jumped as high as he could. With his head above the leaves and
stringy corn tassels, he scanned the field for Grace's little red wings.

At first he saw nothing. So he ran some more and
he jumped again. Running and jumping, all the way down
the row he went~a-running and a-jumping!

He went up the next row and did the same thing, again and again
and again. Seventy-two rows, but Grace was nowhere in that field.

The wind must have carried her even farther away.

Who knew

how far.

It was getting late in the day by then.
Charlie wondered if he ought to give up.

Inside his head, Charlie heard a little voice say, "What's one little butterfly anyway? After all, you've still got ninety-nine back home. Why don't you give up?"

Charlie thought about his little Grace and how he loved her. She was much more important than just "one little butterfly."

So Charlie said a little prayer, took a deep breath, and began to make his way up the tall hill in front of him.

The hill was so steep that Charlie had to climb it like a monkey.
But he didn't realize that dozing at the top was a great, big bull.

Even when the bull's pointy horns came into view,
Charlie was still determined to climb up and stand
on the rock outcrop. He needed to get a better viewpoint
to look for Grace. But just to be safe, he climbed very, very slowly.
And as he drew closer to the bull he barely breathed.
"Easy, boy," he said soothingly. "Easy does it, boy."

Now, it wasn't Charlie who woke that old bull up. No, it was
that pesky horsefly, who up until now had been taking a nap.
But just as Charlie reached the top of the hill, that ornery horsefly
decided to take a bite right out of the bull's nose.

The earth shook as the enraged bull jumped to his hooves.
He jerked his big horned head from side to side trying
to shake off the fly. Then the angry bull spotted Charlie.
Poor Charlie, his feet were frozen just a few feet from the bull.

Before he could even blink, Charlie was on flat on his back, trapped beneath the bull's big boulder of a head. And all he could do was look into the bull's wild yellow eyes and smell the bull's awful breath.

Phew!

The bull snorted and roared and kicked up the dirt as he threatened to grind Charlie into the ground like an old cigar butt. Charlie was afraid to move. He was pinned by a four-legged mountain.

I'm going to die! he thought.

Just then Charlie remembered what his father did to angry bulls. So he lifted his arm and with all his might he slammed his fist right into the bull's wet nose.

Splaaat!

The big bull lifted his big head and made a grunt that sounded like "Huh?"

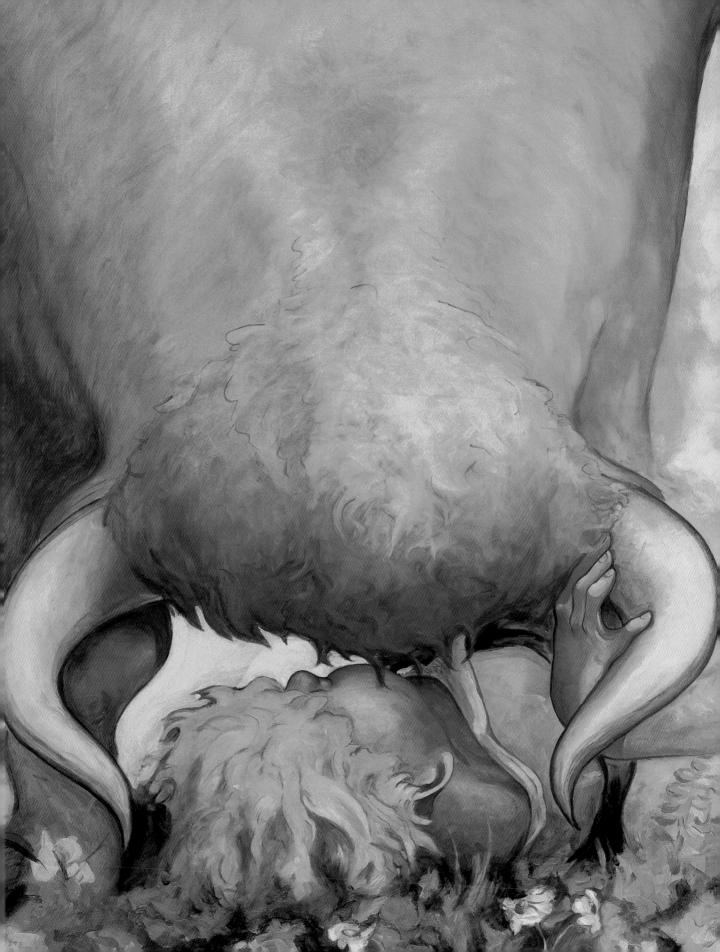

But the stubborn bull didn't move, so Charlie smacked his nose again. Kersplaaat! This time the ground rumbled as the bull jumped away and made a noise that sounded like "Yeeoww!"

The puzzled bull stood a few yards off and sulked, his tail swishing back and forth at the horsefly that had returned to torment him.

Now Charlie's tummy was tied in knots. And to make matters worse, the day's shadows were growing very long. Time was running out. He searched the horizon but did not see a set of red wings anywhere.

"Where are you?" he shouted.

The bull gave him a strange look.

Night would come, and then it would be too late to find her.

Before long, the sun touched the horizon. The windstorm
had softened to a breeze, but poor Grace was nowhere in sight.
Ahead of Charlie lay the thick, dark woods. These woods were his last
chance to find her. Who knew what terrible things might befall her in
the dark of night? She must be so tired and so lonely.
He simply had to find her!

As Charlie went deeper into the woods, sharp twigs and prickly
branches reached out at him, scratching his arms and face.
When a twig jabbed him in the eye he cried out,
"Oww! That smarts!"
Then he continued to walk, covering his sore eye with his hand.

Suddenly Charlie realized that in the dimly lit woods, Grace could
easily be mistaken for a dead leaf. And he sure didn't want to
step on her. So with each step, he lifted his foot high,
and then carefully looked before he planted it safely on the ground.
He knew he looked silly, but he would rather walk funny
than step on dear little Grace.

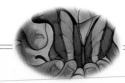

As Charlie moved deeper into the woods, the darkness began to close in around him like a winter overcoat. He had scratches on top of scratches, and his skin now itched something fierce!
He must have brushed against some sort of bad weed.

Finally the woods were so tangled that Charlie could go no farther. He turned his face to the left and was scratched by a briar branch. He looked straight up and was poked by a twig. He looked to the right and a sticky spider's web covered his whole head.

"Grace, where are you?" he cried as he wiped the nasty web from his face. "Where are you? I have to go home now!"

Suddenly Charlie noticed a couple of leaves fluttering down.
He caught them and held them gently. They moved slightly, tickling his palms.
Then Charlie drew his hands up to his face for a closer look.

They were not leaves at all. They were butterfly wings!

It was Grace!

"It's you!" Charlie cried with joy.

She looked so tired, but at last he had Grace safe in his hands!
Their time of fright was over; Charlie had found her. He watched
Grace snuggle up in the palms of his hands, yawn, and fall asleep.

Charlie was bursting with happiness. Joy filled him from head to toe.
"I found you! I found you! I found you!" he sang
at the top of his lungs. His voice echoed throughout the woods.
It shook the branches and rustled the leaves. The squirrels
began to chatter. The birds chirped and squawked. And soon the
whole woods became one big noisy riot.

Charlie smiled down upon his dear little Grace and whispered,
"Let's you and I get home, Grace. It's very late!"

And he carried her all the way home.

Back home, all the butterflies leaped into the air for joy when
Charlie carried Grace into the house. By now she was feeling much,
much better. She was almost her old self again.

They all stayed up late into the night. They laughed and sang
and played fun games to celebrate Grace's return.
Because Grace once was lost, but now she was found.

The Lord rescued me
because he delighted in me.

PSALM 18:19

David Erickson is a talented storyteller who loves inspiring
children to think of Jesus. He has taught, coached, and counseled
middle school students for years, and taught himself to
paint with oils. Now David's landscapes and portraits can be seen
in galleries across his state and have been commissioned for
private collections. Story illustration, inspired by prayer,
is his artistic passion. David and his wife, Monica, enjoy photography,
volleyball, and sketching. They live in Chatfield, Minnesota.